FIGHT OF YOUR LIFE

Fight with Faith

NOVEMBER 10, 2018
WOMEN OF DISTINCTION
Women Making a Difference

Copyright © 2018 by Reach The Press Publishing

All rights reserved. No part of this publication may be reproduced, distributed, or transmitted in any form or by any means, including photocopying, recording, or other electronic or mechanical methods, without the prior written permission of the publisher, except in the case of brief quotations embodied in critical reviews and certain other noncommercial uses permitted by copyright law. For permission requests, write to the publisher, addressed "Attention: Permissions Coordinator," at the address below.

> Reach The Press Publishing
> 14051Belle Chasse Blvd Unit 213
> Laurel, Maryland 20707

Printed in the United States of America

Carolyn A. Ayers

THANK YOU

Jesus, for the time that is given to me to spend with my mother. My Mother sacrificed her body, sleep, social life for me. My mother made sure I had spending money, clothing to wear and a place to sleep. My mother was patience, energetic and shown me love! My mother is far more precious than jewels. This time with her is a gift from god...with My mother Josephine Gilbert Ayers

SPECIAL THANK YOU

TO:
PASTOR EDWARD OLDS AND
FIRST LADY SHEILAH OLDS

PASTOR DEVIN STEPHENSON
AND
FIRST LADY MYA STEPHENSON

I REALLY APPRECIATE YOUR SUPPORT FOR MY OUTREACH MINISTRY

Much Love
Your Sister in Christ

FIGHT OF YOUR LIFE

This book is devoted to all of those who feel that life can't change for them and the Addictions that plague their life

They will never be free from it

Through the power of the Almighty God take back your life and reach your destiny

Love

Your Sister in Christ Jesus

Fight of Your Life

GOD IS UP TO SOMETHING GREAT OR THE DEVIL
WOULDN'T BE FIGHTING YOU THIS HARD
YOU'RE GOING TO WIN

TABLE OF CONTENTS

Acknowledgments   11

Forward   14

Fighting with Faith   28

Fight of Your Life   39

Fight the Good Fight of Faith   45

God Fight the Battle   51

Over Come Guilt   60

The truth set You Free   65

TABLE OF CONTENTS

Tearing Down Stronghold   75

Armed for Battle   100

The Shield for Spiritual Battle   108

Intercession 117

Salvation through the 120
Blood of Jesus

God Can Deliver 124

Dedication 126

ACKNOWLEDGMENTS

To my Lord and Savior, Jesus Christ;

Thank you for entrusting me to deliver this literary treasure, and for giving me Prophet Michael Allen Ayers Sr., First Lady Charlene R. Ayers, Pastor Wilbert Ayers Jr., and Co-Pastor Debra Ayers for prayers and spiritual guidance. I am forever grateful to be blessed with a loving and supportive family who continues to be my strength and inspiration: My mother Mrs. Josephine Ayers, a Prayer Warrior and Intercessor; my sister Evangelist Wanda Denise Ayers.

ACKNOWLEDGMENTS

my daughters and their husbands, Prophetess Lakiesha and Robert Thomas, Sr., Prophetess Quiana, and Minister Cedric Wingard, and La'Shone and Marques Anderson, Sr.; and my son and his wife, Allen II and Shenelle Tillman.

Finally, I want to acknowledge the nine wonderful grandkids that the Lord has blessed me with: Robert Jr., Ronnie, Royal, and Rhea Thomas, Marques Jr., Markel, and Mariah Anderson, Christian S. Tillman and Chloe L. Wingard.

Reach for it. Push yourself as far as you can.

PRAY

UNTIL

SOMETHING

HAPPEN

FORWARD

Fight! The Lord will fight for you; you need only to be still. **Exodus 14:14** The LORD your God, who is going before you, will fight for you, as he did for you in Egypt, before your very eyes, **Deuteronomy 1:30**. I know that many of you will say I was not there to see the great move of God in Egypt. I want you to know that every time you pick up your bible the awesome anointed power of God is before you. **John 1:1**, in the beginning, was the Word and the Word was with God, and the Word was God. Then you replied, "We have sinned against the LORD. We will go up and fight, as the LORD our GOD commanded us." So every one of you put on his weapons, thinking it is easy to go up into the hill country. **Deuteronomy 1:41**. I know that the fight is hard when your mind is telling your body that you're addicted to whatever your inner demon is and that is the problem it's in your mind you have to release those thoughts from your inner thoughts to be free. When you take the mask off the thoughts that Satan planted that are hidden behind the mask and see the Truth. Then you will know the truth, and the truth will set you free. **John 8:32.** Satan no longer has the rights and privileges that you have if you only believe. That is why he does his best to deceive you by planting (depositing) all of the unclean acts for you to commit and make you feel that you have no control and you have to act upon these thoughts. If you take the mask off of Satan you can clearly (without a doubt) see his demonic traits and how ugly they really are. **Trait** refers to some of the characteristics of Satan are murder, liar, jealousy, lust, and thieves just to name a few. Probably most of us would rather speak about the Lord Jesus than about His enemy (and our enemy) the devil, but the Bible says that the devil is a very real and a very dangerous character. Therefore we must speak about him. One of Satan's cunning schemes is to try and convince people that he does not really exist. Satan is often made out to be a joke, but in reality, he should be feared. The devil is a spiritual being just as real as God. He is not as powerful as God, but he is just as real. Jesus said to Peter, "Behold, Satan hath desired to have you, that **he** may sift you as wheat" **Luke 22:31.** Later, the Apostle Peter said, "Be sober, be vigilant, because of your adversary the devil, as a roaring lion, walketh about, seeking whom **he** may devour" **1 Peter 5:8.** According to the Bible, the devil is a created, personal, spirit being. And just because we cannot see him does not mean that he is not real. The Bible indicates that Satan was one of the most magnificent creatures ever created; he was the climax of God's creative wisdom; he was not always the malicious character we know him to be today; he was once a beautiful angel. The Scriptures say (of Lucifer), "Thou was perfect in thy ways from the day that thou was created, till iniquity was found in thee" **Ezekiel 28:15.** Those who believe the message of the Bible believe that there is a real, created, personal devil who is the enemy of God and the enemy of God's people. We don't understand all there is to know about the devil, but the Bible says he has his own synagogue **Revelation 2:9,** his own gospel **Galatians 1:6-9,** his own ministers **2 Corinthians 11:14-15,** his own doctrines **1 Timothy 4:1,** and his own communion service **1 Corinthians 10:2021.** Satan will do all he can to bring defeat into our lives. He is constantly battling for the soul of the sinner and for the life of the saint. The devil's work is to deceive human beings, and he has many subtle devices and many cunning ways by which he does the job. We do well to take seriously the advice of the Apostle Paul when he says in **2 Corinthians 2:11** that we are not to be ignorant of his devices. Jesus says that the devil "abode not in the truth because there is no truth in him. When he speaketh a lie, he speaketh of his own, for he is a liar, and the father of it"

John 8:44. God's truth is revealed in the Bible. Whenever a person tries to question or to argue away any of the teachings of the Bible, you can be sure that it is the old serpent, the devil, trying to deceive that individual. Often Satan tries to accomplish his goal by taking a passage out of its context. One of the most beautiful promises in the New Testament is found in **verse 19 of Philippians 4**. Sometimes Satan quotes from the Bible (he uses Bible verses), but he distorts the truth to try and make the Bible say something altogether different from its obvious statements. The point is that the devil is a liar— and any attempt to play down (or to twist) the Scriptures are definitely motivated by the devil in his attempt to try and dishonor the plan of God. Satan is always on the alert. He is looking for weak places in our defense system; he is eager to take advantage of any opening we might give him through a lack of watchfulness. The Bible speaks of the betrayal of Jesus (just before His crucifixion), and says, "The devil having now put into the heart of Judas Iscariot, Simon's son, to betray him. . . " **John 13:2.** And at another place, the Scripture says, "Ananias, why hath Satan filled thine heart to lie to the Holy Ghost?" **Acts 5:3.** If we would only recognize that the evil temptations which we get from time to time are promoted by a real personal devil who is trying to bring defeat to our souls, we would do more to resist his onslaughts! It is the devil who entices us to do wrong. It is the devil who inflames the passions, and stirs the appetites, and awakens old habits. We don't have to give in to him. We are given the power of choice. But Satan is one who sneaks into the hearts of people and tries to lead all of us astray. The wicked thoughts we contend with from time to time are energized by the devil and empowered by all the forces of evil. The ultimate aim of the devil is to mar us and scar us; to disfigure the image of God in us; to saturate our minds with filth and dirt and moral rot; to wrap us in darkness and lock us forever in the place where there is only weeping and gnashing of teeth. The devil aims to slay everything that is noble and decent and good in our lives. He has energized every rotten deed that has ever been committed by every person that has ever walked on the face of the earth. The devil puts evil suggestions into our minds. The devil has never had a good word to say about God's people. He dislikes us because we love the Lord, and so he tries his best to get us to ruin our testimony by showing enmity toward our fellow-Christians. The Bible says, "But if ye have bitter envying and strife in your hearts, glory not . . . this wisdom descendent not from above but is earthly, sensual, devilish" **James 3:14-15**. The Bible says that a bitter and unforgiving spirit among fellow-Christians is demonic; it is of the devil; it is inspired by Satan. Satan delights in hearing us say unkind and critical (and often untrue) things about our brothers and sisters in Christ. Sharpness and contention among Christians do not promote the cause of Christ. Such conduct helps instead to extend the devil's kingdom. We need to take seriously the warning of **Ephesians 4:32**, where we read, "Be ye kind one to another, tenderhearted, forgiving one another, even as God for Christ's sake hath forgiven you."

The word "kindness" speaks of a generous and thoughtful attitude toward others. The word "tenderhearted" means heartfelt compassion, a sense of sympathy that feels for the needs and the circumstances of others. We should be careful not to quickly bash others with words of negative criticism. Satan, by way of contrast, stirs up bitterness and envy and does everything he can to break down a spirit of harmony among God's people. The devil sows tares of conflict and discontent among believers in order to dampen their testimony. Satan is the one who tempts you to commit sexual immorality. The devil in order to break down the sanctity of our homes and to saturate our communities with fornication and incest and prostitution and adultery and all the other ugly sins related to sexual immorality.

Each of us is confronted daily with the snares, the tactics, the tricks, and the devices of the devil. Satan is not in Hell now; he is not locked up in the bottomless pit (as he will be someday). He is the "god of this age," walking up and down in this world, seeking to drag men and women away from Christ. He has each of our names on his list, and he is doing his level best to drag each one of us down to defeat and destruction. It seems that Satan is working overtime in these days because he knows that his time is limited, and he is aware that shortly he will be cast into the Lake of Fire where he will be tormented day and night forever and ever. See **Revelation 20:10**. We cannot resist the devil in our own human power. We must be a committed child of God and have the Lord Jesus Christ dwelling within. The message to Christian believers in **1 John 4:4** is this: "Greater is he that is in you than he that is in the world." Do you remember the great passage in **Galatians 2:20**? The Apostle Paul says, "I am crucified with Christ; nevertheless I live; yet not I, **but Christ lives in me**." Jesus Christ, who dwells within the body of the believing Christian, is greater than the devil, who is the god of this world! The devil is a supernatural being, and it takes a supernatural power to respond to his devices. Jesus Christ is that power. In order to overcome the devices of the devil, we must surrender our lives to God and receive Jesus into our hearts by faith. When a person takes that step, he becomes a new creature with new desires and with new powers to overcome temptation. We can resist the devil in the same way that Jesus resisted him when He was tempted in the wilderness. Jesus resisted the devil by appealing to the Scriptures. When the devil commanded Him to turn stones into bread, Jesus said, "It is written, man shall not live by bread alone." When the devil told Him to jump off the pinnacle of the Temple, Jesus said, "It is written, Thou shalt not tempt the Lord thy God." When Satan offered Him all the kingdoms of the world, Jesus said, "It is written, Thou shalt worship the Lord thy God, and him only shalt thou serve." Jesus resisted the devil by appealing to the Scriptures. He could have summoned ten thousand angels; He could have displayed His own supernatural powers, but instead, Jesus used the same weapon that is available to every one of us—the Word of God. All of us must make new commitments to spend more time with the Bible; to memorize portions of Scripture; to study the Word of God—so that we will have a Scriptural dart to throw at the devil every time he comes our way with a temptation. One who takes Christ as his Savior and starts to live and work for Him will soon discover that there is an enemy seeking to destroy his faith and testimony. All of us find that living the Christian life involves ongoing Warfare. But God has provided spiritual armor to protect us, and he has placed in our hands a sword—the Word of God— to help us conquer and overcome evil. We read about the armor in **Ephesians 6:10-18**. The armor includes a belt of truth (it always pays to believe the truth), a breastplate of righteousness (the ability to do the right thing), and a shield of faith (the willingness to trust and believe that God Word is true). In addition, He gives the sword of the Spirit which is the Word of God. In the Christian life, we battle against powerful evil forces headed by Satan. To withstand his attacks, we must depend on God's strength and use every piece of armor which is provided. All believers are special objects of Satan's attacks because they are no longer on Satan's side. We need supernatural power to defeat Satan, and God has provided that power by the Holy Spirit who lives within us, and by the provision of armor which surrounds us. May God help every believer to be alert to these truths? For an overseer, as God's steward, must be above reproach. He must not be arrogant or quick-tempered or a drunkard or violent or greedy for gain, **Titus 1:7,** finally, be strong in the Lord and in the strength of his might. Put on the whole armor of God that you may be able to stand against the schemes of the devil. For we do not wrestle against flesh and blood, but against the rulers, against the authorities, against the cosmic powers over this present darkness, against the spiritual forces of evil in the heavenly places. **Ephesians 6:10-12.**

Hebrew 11:6

Fighting with Faith

To fight and destroy demons you must have faith **(Mt 17:19-20)** Then the disciples approached Jesus in private and said, 'Why could we not drive out (a demon)?' He said to them, 'Because of your little faith. Jesus said I say to you, if you have faith the size of a mustard seed, you will say to this mountain, "Move from here to there," and it will move. Nothing will be impossible for you.'" Jesus is telling you, my brother and sister, that if you only believe that His power is greater than any of the demonic forces that Satan has tried to place a stronghold on your life.

That stronghold can be destroyed by your faith if you only believe. **Your faith must have works (Jas 2:14-18)** "What good is it, my brothers and sisters, if someone says he has faith but does not have works? Can that faith save him? If a brother or sister has no money for food for the day, and one of you says to them, 'Go in peace, keep warm and eat well,' but you do not give them the necessities of the body, what good is it? So faith in itself, if it does not have works, it is dead. You can't demonstrate your faith without works, you have to demonstrate your faith by acting upon the very thing you feel you can't be free from by working at breaking free from whatever it is." Your stronghold could be drugs, drinking, lying, and lust just to name a few you know what your fight is.

"**James** does not imply the possibility of **true faith** existing apart from deeds, but merely claim it is impossible to have faith without works. **James** is saying by faith the free acceptance of God's saving revelation. ... By 'works' is meant the obedient implementation of God's revealed will in every aspect of your life. ... Note that **James** is saying if you live according to God's Word and His will in every aspect of your life, you're living your life by faith your faith will make you whole. **Conquer Fear by Faith**
Yes, we can "conquer" our fears, but — surprise! — There will be new ones popping up just around the corner. In a similar way, we can act on faith and, through the grace of God, accomplish things we never thought possible. But again — surprise! — There will be

more God-given invitations to do something new. Challenging. Seemingly impossible. Or to be more blunt, stuff that just seems crazy. How can God possibly think I can? That is when you can put your faith to work by conquering your fear with faith. **Romans 8:31-39** What, then, shall we say in response to these things? If God is for us, who can be against us? He who did not spare his own Son, but gave him up for us all—how will he not also, along with him, graciously give us all things? Who will bring any charge against those whom God has chosen? It is God who justifies. Who then is the one who condemns? No one. Christ Jesus who died—more than that, who was raised from the dead—is at the right hand of God and is also interceding for us.

Who shall separate us from the love of Christ? Shall trouble or hardship or persecution or famine or nakedness or danger or sword? No, in all these things we are **more than conquerors** through him who loved us. For I am convinced that neither death nor life, neither angels nor demons, neither the present nor the future, nor any powers, neither height nor depth, nor anything else in all creation, will be able to separate us from the love of God that is in Christ Jesus our Lord. **Fear over Faith** Consider the apostles: When Jesus said, "Come and follow me." And they did. They stepped away from the lives they were living and went with Jesus. They were taught by him for three years, witnessed miracles and came to believe he was the Messiah.

He is! The Son of God. And yet, they scattered in fear when Our Lord was arrested on the evening of the Holy Thursday. And except for John, they were nowhere to be seen on Good Friday. (Actually, Peter was around early that morning, but he repeatedly claimed, "I don't know the man.") Faith and fear. On that day, for all but John, fear won. Do not let fear and doubt keep you from fighting the Good Fight of Faith. **Faith over Fear** What about Pentecost? Very good question. When the Twelve Apostle came together in prayer and had faith that steamrolled over fear. **Acts 1:12-14** The Upper Room Prayer Meeting: Then they returned to Jerusalem from the mount called Olivet, which is near Jerusalem, a Sabbath day's journey. And when they had entered, they went up into the upper room where they were staying: Peter, James, John, and Andrew; Philip and Thomas; Bartholomew and Matthew; James and Simon; and Judas the son of James. These all continued with one accord in prayer and supplication, with the women and Mary the mother of Jesus, and with His brothers. All who was in the Upper Room believed on one accord in the power of an Almighty God. That is how you can steamroll over fear, destroying doubt and unbelieve by believing and having faith in the power of God who can set you free.

"We must not fear challenges." No. Do not be afraid. We must instead fear faith without challenges, a life without obstacles and pitfalls can't show forth or demonstrate true faith in the power of God. So when someone considers its faith complete and all complete: it does not need to believe in the power of a risen Savior, all is done and finish on the cross. his faith is so watered down that it is useless. We must be afraid of this." Do not fear challenges in life because you have a **Conquering King Christ Jesus who took all power from Satan** and can make you victorious in any challenge that life brings your way.

What about "fear of the Lord"? Fear is "one of the seven gifts of the Holy Spirit that ensures our reverence before God." The **Seven gifts of the Holy Spirit** They are wisdom, understanding, counsel, fortitude, knowledge, piety, and fear of the Lord. "We do not render true service to God so long as we obey from fear and not from love (reverence)." Maturely acting on faith isn't based on our concern for God smiting us; its foundation is our love for the God who loved us first. And always will. Perhaps a way of looking at it in human terms is this: We love Jesus with our heart enough to obey His Word and have faith in His power.

Stop and think! Do you have faith to believe that you can be free from lust, drugs, drinking, and homosexuality? If you have faith in the power of Jesus Christ you can be set free.

WOMEN OF DISTINCTION

CAROLYN A. AYERS

Faith is Power

Fight of Your Life

Whatever your fight is drugs, drinking, lust and adultery, fornication, lying one or more of these. Your addiction, it could not be one of these but whatever your inner demon may be. As the definition states addiction is a brain disorder characterized by compulsive engagement in inducements, despite adverse consequences. The property that characterizes addictive stimuli is that they are reinforcing (i.e., they increase the likelihood that a person will seek repeated exposure. This implies that the person has no control of their own life that their addiction is forcing and controlling their every move.

What I want you to understand that the fight is not a physical fight as the clinicians in this world would have you believe. This is a spiritual fight that affects the heart of your mind. It is affecting your inner being your soul which is your mind. Without breath, there is no life and therefore there are no thoughts.

> **And the LORD God formed man of the dust of the ground, and breathed into his nostrils the breath of life; and man Became a living soul. Genesis 2:7**

For the weapons of our warfare are not carnal, but mighty through God to the pulling down of strongholds; Casting down imaginations, and every high thing that exalteth itself against the knowledge of God, and bringing into captivity every thought to the obedience of Christ; **2 Corinthians 10:4-5** My brother my sister do not let Satan fool you with his deceptive persuasion that gives you the false hope that the Love of Christ Jesus will overlook your sins and you will still abide with Him in his Kingdom. I want you to know the truth if you did not know…… Or do you not know that the unrighteous will not inherit the kingdom of God? Do not be deceived: neither the sexually immoral, nor idolaters, nor adulterers, nor those who practice homosexuality, nor thieves, nor the greedy, nor drunkards, nor revilers, nor swindlers will inherit the kingdom of God. **1 Corinthians 6:9-10** therefore, submit to God. Resist the devil and he will flee from you." **James 4:7** I'm telling you that you're in the fight of your life and you have to denounce any thoughts that the devil tries to plague your mind with. "If you walk in the Lord statutes and keep His commandments, and perform them ... you shall eat your bread to the full, and dwell in your land safely. You will chase your enemies, and they shall fall by the sword before you. Five of you shall chase a hundred, and a hundred of you shall put ten thousand to flight; your enemies shall fall by the sword before you." **Leviticus 26:**8 the more that you resist the devil you're taking back control of your life and walking into your destiny. Stop letting the devil lie to you telling you that you cannot be free from your addiction because that is just a plot and plan to steal your soul. The devil knows that you have all control because the breath of the Almighty God is living inside of you and giving you life. The devil tries to deceive and use deception propagating beliefs in things that are not true. Like giving you thoughts that make you feel that you cannot be free from your inner demon. "For the Lord your God walks in the midst of your camp, to deliver you and give your enemies over to you; therefore your camp shall be holy, that He may see no unclean thing among you, and turn away from you." **Deuteronomy 23:14.**

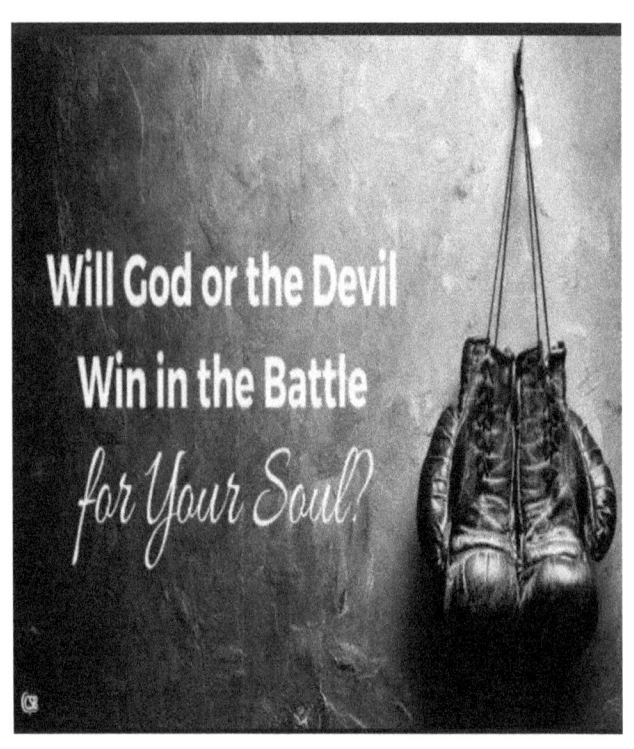

Fight the Good Fight of Faith

Then the LORD God formed a man from the dust of the ground and breathed into his nostrils the breath of life, and the man became a living (being) Soul. **Genesis 2:7** the breathed that you breath is God himself that gives you power to Fight the Good Fight of Faith. The Word was God from the beginning; The Word Became Flesh; in the beginning was the Word, and the Word was with God, and the Word was God. The Word of God increases your faith by the account of his miraculous powers.

This book The Fight of Your Life is a practical, helpful resource that is specially designed to help new and growing Christians become effective disciples/warriors of Christ, and is built entirely on the Word of God as told in the Scriptures. Fight the good fight of faith. Take hold of the eternal life to which you were called when you made your good confession in the presence of many witnesses. In the sight of God, who gives life to everything, and of Christ Jesus, who while testifying before Pontius Pilate made the good confession, I charge you to keep this command without spot or blame until the appearing of our LORD Jesus Christ, which God will bring about in his own time. God, the blessed and only Ruler, the King of Kings and Lord of Lords, **1 Timothy 6:12-15.**

2Timothy 4:7-8 I have fought the good fight, I have finished the race, and I have kept the faith. Now there is in store for me the crown of righteousness, which the LORD, the righteous Judge, will award to me on that day and not only to me but also to all who have longed for his appearing. **Galatians 5:16-18** So, I say, walk by the Spirit, and you will not gratify the desires of the flesh. For the flesh desires what is contrary to the Spirit and the Spirit what is contrary to the flesh. They are in conflict with each other so that you are not to do whatever you want. But if you are led by the Spirit, you are not under the law. **Ephesians 6:13-15** Therefore put on the full armor of God, so that when the day of evil comes, you may be able to stand your ground, and after you have done everything, to stand. Stand firm then, with the belt of truth buckled around your waist, with the breastplate of righteousness in place, and with your feet fitted with the readiness that comes from the gospel of peace. When your faith is little the devil can rip it out. **James 1:12** Let us not become weary in doing well, for at the proper time we will reap a harvest if we do not give up. **Galatians 6:9** who gave himself for our sins to rescue us from the present evil age, according to the will of our God and Father, **Galatians 1:4** so do not throw away your confidence; it will be richly rewarded. You need to persevere so that when you have done the will of God, you will receive what he has promised. **Hebrews 10:3536** For I know the plans I have for you," declares the LORD, "plans to prosper you and not to harm you, plans to give you hope and a future.

Jeremiah 29:11 the one who does what is sinful is of the devil because the devil has been sinning from the beginning. The reason the Son of God appeared was to destroy the devil's work. **1 John 3:8** for I am convinced that neither death nor life, neither angels nor demons, neither the present nor the future, nor any powers, neither height nor depth, nor anything else in all creation, will be able to separate us from the love of God that is in Christ Jesus our LORD. **Romans 8:38-39**

> The God of peace will soon crush Satan under your feet. The grace of our Lord Jesus be with you.
>
> **Romans 16:20**

SATAN IS UNDER YOUR FEET

God Fight the Battle

The Lord is a Man of War; the Lord is His name ... Your Right Hand, O Lord, has become glorious in power; Your right hand. O Lord has dashed the enemy in pieces. And in the greatness of your excellence, you have overthrown those who rose against your children; you sent forth your wrath which consumed them like stubble." **Exodus 15:3, 6** "The Lord shall go forth like a mighty Man; He shall stir up His zeal like a Man of War. He shall cry out, yes, shout aloud; He shall prevail against His enemies." **Isaiah 42:13** "I will go before you and make the crooked paths straight; I will break in pieces the gates of bronze and cut the bars of iron." **Isaiah 45:2** "For you shall not go out with haste, nor go by flight; for the Lord will go before you, and the God of Israel will be your rear guard." **Isaiah 52:12** "Therefore understand today the Lord your God is He who goes before you as a consuming fire. He will destroy them and bring them down before you; so you shall drive them out and destroy them quickly, as the Lord has said to you." **Deuteronomy 9:3** "The Lord will fight for you, and you shall hold your peace." **Exodus 14:14** "Be strong and courageous; do not be afraid nor dismayed before the king of Assyria, nor before all the multitude that is with him; for there are more with us than with him. With him is an arm of flesh; but with us is the Lord our God, to help us and to fight our battles." **2 Chronicles 32:7** "... For I will contend with him who contends with you." **Isaiah 49:25** "... Since it is a righteous thing with God to repay with tribulation those who trouble you." **2**

Thessalonians 1:6 "The eternal God is your refuge, and underneath are the everlasting arms; He will thrust out the enemy from before you, and will say, 'destroy!' **Deuteronomy 33:27** do not say, "I will recompense evil," wait for the Lord, and He will save you." **Proverbs 20:22** "I will bless those who bless you, and I will curse those who curse you." **Genesis 12:3** "Many a time they have afflicted me from my youth; yet they have not prevailed against me … The Lord is righteous; He has cut in pieces the cords of the wicked." **Psalm 129:2** "It is God who avenges me, and subdues the peoples under me; He delivers me from my enemies. You also lift me up above those who rise against me; you have delivered me from the violent man." **Psalm 18:47** "Plead my cause, O Lord, with those who strive with me; fight against those who fight against me. Take hold of shield and buckler, and stand up for my help. Also, draw out the spear, and stop those who pursue me. Say to my soul, "I am your salvation." **Psalm 35:1** "When my enemies turn back, they shall fall and perish at your presence. For you have maintained my right hand and my cause; you sat on the throne judging in righteousness." **Psalm 9:3** "Do not be afraid of their faces, for I am with you to deliver you," says the Lord. **Jeremiah 1:8** "God is a just judge, and God is angry with the wicked every day. If He does not turn back, He will sharpen His sword; He bends His bow and makes it ready. He prepares for Himself instruments of death; He makes His arrows into fiery shafts." **Psalm 7:11** "He will guard the feet of His saints, but the wicked shall be silent in darkness. For by strength no man shall prevail. The adversaries of the Lord shall be broken in pieces; from heaven, He will thunder against them. The Lord will judge the ends of the earth. He will give strength to His king, and exalt the horn of His anointed. **1 Samuel 2:9** "... For we have no power against this great multitude that is coming against us; nor do we know what to do, but our eyes are upon You ... Then the Spirit of the Lord came upon Jahaziel ... thus says the Lord to you: 'Do not be afraid nor dismayed because of this great multitude, for the battle is not yours, but God's ... You will not need to fight in this battle. Position yourselves, stand still and see the salvation of the Lord, who is with you, O Judah and Jerusalem!" Do not fear or be dismayed; tomorrow go out against them, for the Lord is with you."

2 Chronicles 20:12-17 "Behold, all those who were incensed against you shall be ashamed and disgraced; they shall be as nothing, and those who strive with you shall perish. You shall seek them and not find them – those who contend with you. Those who war against you shall be as nothing, as a nonexistent thing. For I, the Lord your God will hold your right hand, saying to you, 'Fear not, I will help you.' " **Isaiah 41:11** "When the enemy comes in like a flood, the Spirit of the Lord will lift up a standard against him." **Isaiah 59:19** "Now I know that the Lord saves His anointed; He will answer him from His holy heaven with the saving strength of His right hand." **Psalm 20:6** "Though I walk in the midst of trouble, you will revive me; you will stretch out your hand against the wrath of my enemies, and your right hand will save me.

The Lord will perfect that which concerns me ..." **Psalm 138:7** "When you pass through the waters, I will be with you; and through the rivers, they shall not overflow you. When you walk through the fire, you shall not be burned, nor shall the flame scorch you." **Isaiah 43:2** "For they did not gain possession of the land by their own sword, nor did their arm save them; but it was your right hand, your arm, and the light of your countenance because you favored them." **Psalm 44:3** "You marched through the land in indignation; You trampled the nations in anger. You went forth for the salvation of your people, for salvation with your anointed. You struck the head from the house of the wicked." **Habakkuk 3:12** "The righteous cry out, and the Lord hears, and delivers them out of all their troubles."

Psalm 34:17 "And I commanded Joshua at that time, saying, 'Your eyes have seen all that the Lord Your God has done to these two kings; so will the Lord do to all the kingdoms through which you pass. You must not fear them, for the Lord Your God Himself fights for you.' "
Deuteronomy 3:21

There is power in the name of Jesus to break every chain.

Over Come Guilt

Guilt plagues everyone to some degree, for we all have to lay our heads on our pillow at night and accept the fact that we have not done as well as we could have done. Guilt is the most difficult problem in the whole realm of psychological therapy because sometimes it is hard for one to forgive him or herself. This makes it so hard because you have to forgive yourself before you can forgive someone else. Forgiveness is the first step to winning the fight. When the devil knows that he cannot haunt you with the mistakes of your past and your current mistakes he has no hold on you.

Guilt has been a problem since the beginning of time as we read our bible it tells us of mistakes that were made that lead to guilt. It was guilt that caused Adam and Eve to hide when God came walking in the cool of the day. **Genesis 3:8** it was guilt over his adulterous affair that caused David to say, "When I kept silent, my bones wasted away from my groaning all day long." **Psalm 32:3** It was guilt that caused Isaiah to cry out "Woe is me for I am a man with unclean lips" when he came into the presence of the Living God. **Isaiah 6:5** When the Pharisees brought the woman caught in adultery, Jesus looked at the angry mob and said, "If anyone of you is without sin, let him be the first to through a stone at her."

It was guilt that caused the men to drop their stones, one by one, and walk away. **John 8:14** It was guilt that caused Judas Iscariot to take his own life after he betrayed Jesus in the Garden of Gethsemane. **Matthew 27:5** And Guilt continue to haunt the human race. But I want you to know this; there is therefore now no condemnation to them which are in Christ Jesus, who walk not after the flesh but after the Spirit. **Roman 8:1** for if our heart condemns us, God is greater than our heart, and knoweth all things. **1 John 3:20**. So, when you ask Jesus Christ to forgive your sins Christ throw them in the sea of forgetfulness and that is where you must throw guilt. When Satan try to bring up your past and the mistakes that you made let him know. **Ephesians 1:7** in him we have redemption through his blood, the forgiveness of sins, in accordance with the riches of God's grace. Hebrew 10: 19-22Therefore, brothers and sisters since we have confidence to enter the most Holy Place by the blood of Jesus. By a new and living way opened for us through the curtain, that is, his body, and since we have a great priest over the house of God. Let us draw near to God with a sincere heart in full assurance of faith, having our heart sprinkled to cleanse us from a guilty conscience and having our bodies washed with pure water.

> By faith, take back everything the enemy has stolen from you.

The truth set You Free

The most challenging questions Men of God and Women of God must answer are these: "How can I present God's Word in a way that will accomplish the most good? Is my disposition regarding truth and my attitude toward others such that the cause of Christ is helped, or hindered?" **Ephesians 4:15** provides the key to answering these questions: ". . . But speaking the truth in love may grow up into him in all things, which is the head, even Christ. . . Feeble, arrogant men are often tempted by their own conceit to pose the question which Pilate asked in **John 18:38**, "What is the truth?" Pilate scoffed at the very concept of absolute truth. By his question, he implies that all things are relative. Contrary to Pilate's appraisal, Jesus affirms that his teaching was based on unbiased truth. "Every one that is of the truth heareth my voice". Christ's teachings do not stem from man's philosophy; they are not the result of personal feelings or prejudice. The Bible tells us in plain language that it is truth and that man can only be saved by humble obedience to that truth in accordance with God's will. "Sanctify them through thy truth," **John 17:17** tells us; "thy word is the truth." **John 8:32** states plainly, "And ye shall know the truth, and the truth shall make you free." Truth is found in **John 14:6**. There is such a thing as absolute, unbiased truth, and Jesus spoke the truth. "I am the way, the truth, and the life: no man cometh unto the Father but by me" **John 14:6**.

Since you and I are to speak the truth, that means we must speak from the Bible. "If any man speaks, let him speak as the revelations of God . . ." **I Pet. 4:11.** It also means that we may not neglect parts of the Bible we should eat the whole Roll and we will find the truth. In the Book of Acts Paul understood the importance of speaking the truth. In **Acts 20:27**, when he tells the elders at Ephesus that "I have not shunned to declare unto you all the counsel of God," he's saying he told them all the truth. God's Word makes man complete **2 Tim. 3:16-17**, so Paul didn't hold back any part of it from them. I'm not saying that the Man of God or Woman of God should preach the whole Bible in every sermon, or else they have lied? No, but like Paul, we must resolve to preach only that which is true, and we can endeavor to examine all that God has revealed on a subject to come to an understanding of the truth. If we neglect part of the truth, if we speak to part of the truth as though it were all, or with a view to deceive, we err. In the Book of Acts, it tells us how we are to speak the truth. We are to speak it in love. This describes our attitude in presenting the truth. While love is an abstract noun we often struggle to understand, I find it easiest to think of acting in another person's best interest. As Christians, we should always remember the love which God and Christ manifested for us. In **Rom. 5:8** we read, "But God commendeth his love toward us, in that, while we were yet sinners, Christ died for us."

God loved us enough to send His son to this earth as the only acceptable, perfect sacrifice for sins. Christ loved us enough to suffer the cruelest kind of death to pay the penalty for our sins. Christ Jesus acted in our best interest. Following the example of Christ, then, we should act in the best interest of others. We don't speak the truth just to win an argument. We don't use the truth like a hammer to hit someone over the head. Love means we don't look for opportunities to show the superiority of our knowledge. We don't use the truth like a harsh spotlight to create unnecessary embarrassment for someone. We speak the truth in love with a view to saving souls. We speak the truth to uplift and comfort the fainthearted. We speak the truth to restore those who have wandered from God and into sin. We speak the truth to instruct and exhort. We speak the truth to encourage and admonish. We speak the truth to correct and persuade. Always, always, we speak the truth to glorify God. Speaking the truth in love is a mark of a mature Christian. By doing this, Paul says, we ". . . may grow up into him in all things, which is the head, even Christ. . . ." Speaking the truth in love is a sign of one who is becoming more Christ-like in his attitude and actions. **Ephesians 4:14** Then we will no longer be infants tossed back and forth by the waves, and blown here and there by every wind of teaching and by the cunning and craftiness of men in their deceitful scheming. **Ephesians 4:15** is not a verse which is difficult to understand, but it is a challenge to practice! I'm going to work on it. I'm sure going to pray about it. I'm going to ask God to grant me spiritual wisdom that I may apply it correctly. Instead, speaking the truth in love, we will grow to become in every respect the mature body of him who is the head, that is, Christ Jesus. **Ephesians 4:15,** May I humbly suggest that it's a special challenge for each one of us as we wrestle with some of the difficult problems of our life? As we struggle with issues and the deity of Christ, let us remember to speak the truth in love. Let us remember that it's not genuine love if we refuse to speak the truth. Oftentimes I'm afraid we use love for brethren as an excuse not to deal directly with a problem. Also, let us remember that it's not the truth as God would have it expressed if love is absent. The mature Christian heeds Paul's full admonition. He speaks the truth in love. The point is, there's a way Christians are to proclaim the truth. Our attitude should reflect the fact that we want to help, not hinder. Is there a time to deal directly, plainly, even forcefully with a problem? Absolutely! In **Titus 3:10** Paul instructs If there is someone around you and they are not lining up with the Word of God in the congregation or your surroundings, you don't tap dance around like you're tiptoeing on hot coals. You get after it and deal with the problem. Show some backbone, before more harm is done! But, love for all the brethren and love for God should be a Christian's attitude toward life, even when we are pressed to make firm stands on difficult matters. Our speech can be direct and bold, with courage and conviction, even as we maintain a Christian's character. As we labor with fellow saints in a local church of Christ, let our attitude be one of loving the truth and loving one another. Let us prefer brother and sister above self. **Phil. 2:3-4.** Let us labor together in the kingdom of our Lord. Humble yourselves, therefore, under God's mighty hand, that he may lift you up in due time. Cast all your anxiety on him because he cares for you. Be alert and of sober mind. Your enemy the devil prowls around like a roaring lion looking for someone to devour**. 1 Peter 5:6-8** on the contrary:

"If your enemy is hungry, feed him; if he is thirsty, give him something to drink. In doing this, you will heap burning coals on his head." Do not be overcome by evil, but overcome evil with good. **Romans 12:20-21**

Tearing Down Stronghold

Spiritual strongholds is found once in the New Testament, used to descript the Christian's spiritual battle: "Though we walk in the flesh, we do not war according to the flesh, for the weapons of our warfare are not of the flesh, but divinely powerful for the destruction of fortresses strongholds **2 Corinthians 10:3-4**. This scripture reveals the following facts about our warfare: Our battle is not planned according to the way this world fights; earthly tricks are not our apprehension. Our weapons are not physical, for our warfare is spiritual in nature.

Rather than guns and daggers, our weapons are those of the "full armor of God" and consist of "the belt of truth buckled around your waist, with the breastplate of righteousness in place, and with your feet fitted with the readiness that comes from the gospel of peace. In addition to all this, take up the shield of faith, with which you can extinguish all the flaming arrows of the devil. Take the helmet of salvation and the sword of the Spirit, which is the Word of God" **(Ephesians 6:1417).** Our power comes from God alone. God's plan is to demolish spiritual strongholds. "We demolish arguments and every posturing that sets itself up against the knowledge of God, and we take captive every thought to make it obedient to Christ" **(2 Corinthians 10:5).**

The "arguments" are the reasoning, and schemes of the demonic forces of this world. The Christian, wearing his spiritual armor and bearing his spiritual weapons, sets out to "conquer" the world for Christ, but he soon finds obstacles. The enemy has constructed strongly fortified garrisons to resist the Truth and prevent God's plan of redemption. There is the fortress of human reasoning, reinforced with many subtle arguments and the pretense of logic. There is the castle (stronghold) of passion, with reinforcements defended by lust, pleasure, and greed. And there is the pinnacle of pride, in which the human heart initiate and revels in thoughts of its own excellence and sufficiency. The enemy is firmly engrained; these strongholds have been guarded for thousands of years, presenting a great wall of resistance to the Truth. None of this frightens the Christian warrior, however. Using the weapons of God's choosing, he attacks the strongholds, and by the miraculous power of Christ, the walls are breached, and the strongholds of sin and error are battered down. The victorious Christian enters the ruins and leads captive, as it were, every false theory and every human viewpoint that had once proudly asserted its independence from God. Sharing the gospel is not the only time we see resistance. We can also face demonic strongholds in our own lives, in our families, and even in our churches. Anyone who has fought an addiction of any kind struggled with pride or had to "flee youthful and adult lusts" knows that sin, a lack of faith, and a worldly outlook on life are indeed

"**Strongholds**." The Lord is building His Church, and the "gates of hell shall not prevail against it" **(Matthew 16:18).** What we need are Christian soldiers, totally surrendered to the will of the Lord of Hosts, who will use the spiritual weapons He provides. That is what I 'm asking you to do join our Army and become a Christian soldier. **What exactly is a stronghold?** A stronghold is an incorrect thinking pattern that has molded itself into our way of thinking. These strongholds have the capability to affect our feelings, how we respond to various situations in life, and they play a large role in our spiritual freedom. Such as the statement once a drug addict always a drug addict this is the false report that worldly philosophy plant in your mind but it is only a tactic to keep you from believing in the power of an

Almighty God. I can go on and on I cannot stop being a prostitute, but I want you to think about your demonic strongholds in your inner self that you need to let go. **Where do strongholds come from?** Strongholds are built upon deception and error. These errors and deceptions which form strongholds can come from a wide variety of sources, including our environment, those around us, our parents or even demon spirits. People have picked up a demon, then the demon quickly builds one or more strongholds in their mind that must be later torn down. **Demonic bondage & strongholds** a person who has a demon behind their stronghold(s) may find it nearly impossible to tear them down and keep down. This is because the demon will be working hard at rebuilding and holding those strongholds in place. They will be countering that person's efforts to tear them down. It will seem as if they are hitting a brick wall, and even if they seem to make progress, it seems like their efforts are in vain because it keeps coming back. If this is the case, then the person likely has a demon which is inside them rebuilding and trying to hold that stronghold in place. The demons should be driven out in Jesus' name, then the stronghold will come down much easier and not be so quick to return.

Call on the name of Jesus and pray without ceasing, Satan cannot over step the power of prayer. How do you tear down strongholds?

Since strongholds are built upon error and falsehood, it is through the truth that you tear down such faulty thinking patterns. Strongholds are built when we accept and receive an error and begin to meditate on them. It forms in our minds what is known as an imagination, that is, a false concept that we believe to be true, but in reality is not. The Bible speaks about these imaginations clearly, and shows us how they can be torn down:

2 Corinthians 10:4, "(For the weapons of our warfare are not carnal, but mighty through God to the pulling down of strongholds ;) <u>Casting down imaginations</u>, and every high thing that exalteth itself against the knowledge of God, and bringing into captivity every thought to the obedience of Christ." The renewing of our minds and strongholds will be destroyed.

We know that strongholds and imaginations must be cast down, but how? By being transformed through the renewing of our minds:

> *Romans 12:2, "And be not conformed to this world: but be ye transformed by the renewing of your mind, that ye may prove what is that good, and acceptable, and perfect, will of God."*

As our minds are renewed, we may prove (discern) what is good, acceptable and perfect, and the will of God. These things are some of the very things that strongholds rise themselves against! Many people who are caught up in shame based thinking do not realize that it's God's will and it is good for them to disassociate themselves from their past. Their minds need to be renewed, and as those strongholds come down they will be able to see God's will and respond. How are our minds renewed and cleansed? Through the washing of the Word, our minds are transformed and strongholds are torn down. Spending time and meditating on the Word of God washes our minds and corrects our false thinking patters (strongholds).

***Ephesians 5:26-27**, "That he might sanctify and cleanse it with the washing of water by the word, That he might present it to himself a glorious church, not having a spot, or wrinkle, or any such thing; but that it should be holy and without blemish."*

As we meditate and wash our minds with God's Word, we will be transformed by the renewing of our minds, and we will come to know the will of God and discern what is right, perfect and good. Our strongholds, which are based on error and deception will not stand a chance as the light of God's Word (truth) is shed upon those areas of our minds. I think too many people make strongholds out to be a complex subject. Strongholds are merely incorrect thinking patterns. They are patterns in our minds that are programmed to think contrary to the truth. For example, a common scenario is where a person feels dirty, guilty and is shameful of their past. They are so used to thinking about their past, that it's driven the person to think and feel like a failure! They feel unworthy to have a close intimate relationship with God, which greatly affects their spiritual strength, faith, and relationship with Him.

No wonder Satan tries to build such strongholds in our minds!

So how does Satan build these strongholds?

He starts by reminding us of our past failures and sins. He brings up things that we ought not to be dwelling upon, and tries to make us agree with him on how badly we failed. We then have the choice to listen and agree with him or listen to God's Word (which is telling us that those sins have been washed away).   If we take the devil's bait and begin to mediate on our failures, it will begin to pull us down spiritually and strongholds will develop. We will begin to see ourselves as failures because we've taken the bait and chose to meditate on a lie that the devil has fed us! It is also not uncommon to find a person who picks up a demonic spirit through sin (such as fornication), and that demon uses its newly gained rights (or ability) in the person's mind to quickly build strongholds. Since the demon is able to influence the person from the inside now, it can get the job done much quicker. This is not an uncommon scenario! Not only does the demonic spirit(s) need to be driven out, but the stronghold also needs to be torn down before the person will experience a complete breakthrough. **Strongholds can and do play a big part of how we feel** If we think we are a failure, we will feel like failures. If you think you're hopeless, you will feel hopeless. If you know you are forgiven, you'll feel clean inside. If you constantly think of your past failures, you will see yourself as associated with them. If you constantly think of how you have been separated from your past when the Blood of Jesus has washed it away, you will feel bright and clean inside. Changing the way you think can make a big difference in the way you feel! **How do we tear down strongholds?** Strongholds are built upon deception and lies that we've accepted into our minds. So how do you counter a lie? How do you counter deception? With the truth. Where do we find the truth? In the Word of God. As we can see in Ephesians, this weapon is known as the sword of the Spirit:

Ephesians 6:17, "...the sword of the Spirit, which is the word of God." In **2 Corinthians**, we are told that our spiritual weaponry is designed to tear down strongholds:

2 Corinthians 10:3-5, "For though we walk in the flesh, we do not war after the flesh: (For the weapons of our warfare are not carnal, but mighty through God to <u>the pulling down of strongholds</u> ;) Casting down imaginations, and every high thing that exalteth itself against the knowledge of God, and bringing into captivity every thought to the obedience of Christ."

This is a great verse that gives us a good idea of how we are to go about tearing down strongholds in our minds. First, since the sword of the Spirit is the offensive piece of our weaponry, it is a great tool for tearing down strongholds. You need to go on the offensive to tear down a stronghold, and the Word of God is the weapon you have to use.
So when the devil tries to tell you, "You really have sinned, haven't you?" Living in Homosexuality and any other form of sin adultery, fornication etc……

Romans 1:26-28 Because of this, God gave them over to shameful lusts. Even their women exchanged natural sexual relations for unnatural ones. In the same way, the men also abandoned natural relations with women and were inflamed with lust for one another. Men committed shameful acts with other men and received in themselves the due penalty for their error. Furthermore, just as they did not think it worthwhile to retain the knowledge of God, so God gave them over to a depraved mind so that they do what ought not to be done. God's timeless Word reveals His plan for humanity and His intentions for marriage and sexuality. **Genesis 1:28** And God blessed man and woman, and God said unto them, be fruitful, and multiply, and replenish the earth. While Scripture teaches that homosexual acts are sinful, these Bible verses aren't about condemning homosexuals, gays, lesbians, or transgender people. Rather, read God's loving warning and offer of grace for all those who have strayed from His will for sex and sinful acts. We live in a fallen world with a fallen nature, but in Christ, we can be new creations by his Love. You need to counter it with, "**1 John 3:5** tells me that the reason Jesus went to the cross was to take away that sin! **Hebrew 8:12** tells me that even God has chosen to forget my sin!" I'm very sure Satan hates that! It reminds him of the days when he tried tempting Jesus: Satan said to Jesus, "If thou be the Son of God, command that these stones be made bread." **Matthew 4:3** But Jesus replied with,"

It is written, Man shall not live by bread alone, but by every word that proceedeth out of the mouth of God." **Matthew 4:4** what did Satan do? After Jesus spoke the Word a few times, he had no choice but to flee... his efforts were useless against Jesus! Jesus knew the relevant scriptures to quote, and took away Satan's ability to influence Him! As we can see, we are told to cast down imaginations. What are imaginations? They are things that we imagine... the devil usually plants them in our minds when he asks us a question that starts out with "What if..." Don't waste your time trying to reason things with the devil. Just throw it out and leave him hanging! Get your mind on God's Word and off of what the devil is trying to tell you. We are to cast down every thought that comes into our minds that opposes the knowledge of God. What is the knowledge of God? Since God associates Himself with His Word **John 1:1**, in the beginning was the Word, and the Word was with God, and the Word was God. If anything comes into our minds that is contrary to God's Word, throw it out! Do not waste your time thinking about it or trying to reason with it. If Satan is trying to tell you that God is not wanting to forgive you, then don't listen to it. Why? Because His Word says otherwise:

Isaiah 30:18, "Therefore the LORD longs to be gracious to you, and therefore He waits on high to have compassion on you."

Not only does He want to forgive your sins, so that your relationship with Him can be restored, He longs (which means He deeply desires) to do so!

One of the last things Satan wants us to know is God's forgiving and loving nature towards us even after we have sinned!

As you can see, strongholds are built on lies and deception. How do you counter such things? With truth! Where do you find truth? In the Word of God! Stop thinking about what Satan has been feeding you, and begin to meditate on God's Word. Take verses in the Bible that run contrary to what the devil's been feeding you, and repeat them to yourself over and over out loud. Think about them often, and meditate on them.

The devil got his stronghold built by causing you to meditate on his lies and deception, so if you want to tear down that stronghold, you need to begin meditating on the exact opposite, which is **God's Word.** Listening to and reasoning with the things the devil puts in your mind is exactly what he wants you to do. It feed his strongholds when you allow your mind to meditate on Satan's word (opposite of God's Word). Cut him off at the source and say NO to the garbage he's been feeding you, and at the same time turn to God's Word. Begin to feed, meditate upon, think about often and dwell upon on the truth. It will stop Satan dead in his tracks! It is also possible to have strongholds in place because demonic spirits have attached themselves to you at some point or another, they need to be driven out. If you work hard at tearing down strongholds by applying the truths in God's Word and this teaching, and yet you seem to hit a wall, it may be because a demonic spirit needs to be driven out. It is very possible (and not uncommon) to experience quite a bit of freedom through applying the principals in this teaching even if there is a demonic spirit present, but you will only go so far and feel like you're hitting a wall. That is a sign of a demon at work that needs to be driven out. It can be awfully hard to battle when they are working on you from the inside out. Resisting them from the outside is easy, but resisting them when they are on the inside can be extremely hard.

If you seem to have reached an immovable mountain, you might want to consider the possibility of needing to have an unclean spirit driven out. At this point in your life you need to surround yourself around powerful prayer warriors.

FIT FOR THE FIGHT
Joshua 1:6-9

Joshua 1:6-9

Be strong and courageous, because you will lead these people to inherit the land I swore to their ancestors to give them. "Be strong and very courageous. Be careful to obey all the law my servant Moses gave you; do not turn from it to the right or to the left, that you may be successful wherever you go. Keep this Book of the Law always on your lips; meditate on it day and night, so that you may be careful to do everything written in it. Then you will be prosperous and successful. Have I not commanded you?

Be strong and courageous. Do not be afraid; do not be discouraged, for the Lord your God will be with you wherever you go."

Arm for Battle

Intercessory prayer is a serious matter. And just like soldiers who are preparing for battle, we cannot take on the enemy if we leave our weapons behind. That's why we must go into "battle" armed for spiritual conflict (see **2 Cor. 10:3, 4**. First, recognize that Jesus is in control of the situation. Jesus "rules over forces, authorities, powers, and rulers ... over all beings in this world and will rule in the future world as well" **Eph. 1:21**. He is King of Kings and Lord of Lords. Then, put on "all the armor God gives" **(see Eph. 6)** so that you will be ready to fight with God's weapons.

These are the "weapons of our warfare" that can pull down strongholds in the spirit world **(see 2 Cor. 10:3, 4).** They will also protect you from the attacks that are sure to come once you begin the spiritual battle. Next, bind the work of Satan, knowing that Jesus has given you authority "to defeat the power of your enemy" **(Luke 10:19)**. If God shows you the identity of specific spiritual strongholds that are at work, take authority over these strongholds in the name of Jesus. And always remember that "God's Spirit is in you and is more powerful than the one that is in the world" **1 John 4:4.**

Finally, as you begin the spiritual battle, take comfort knowing that you are not alone: Jesus also is interceding on your behalf! The Bible says that Jesus "is able to save forever those who draw near to God through Him, since He always lives to make intercession for them" **(Heb. 7:25; see also Romans 8:26, 27, 34).**

PERSIST IN BATTLE

Intercessory prayer is also a prayer that doesn't give up. It's the kind of prayer that endures all setbacks and overcomes every obstacle. Its prayer that "presses on" until we "apprehend" God's will in whatever situation we are facing **(see Phil. 3:12,).** This kind of prayer is the key to seeing breakthroughs in your life and in the lives of those around you.

Jesus gave a great model for intercession in the story of the persistent friend. Here we see a friend who knocks on his neighbor's door at midnight to ask for three loaves of bread. The neighbor does not want to get up, but Jesus said, "because of his friend's persistence he will get up and give him as much as he needs" **Luke 11:8.** Then Jesus said, "Everyone who asks will receive, everyone who searches will find, and the door will be opened for everyone who knocks" **Luke 11:10**. Those words mean to keep on asking, keep on seeking, and keep on knocking. In God's time, your persistence in intercessory prayer will reap a spiritual harvest in your life and the lives of those around you!

BATTLING FOR YOUR NATION
Throughout the Bible, God searched for those willing to fight the spiritual battle for their land. In Ezekiel, God says, "And I searched for a man among them who should build up the wall and stand in the gap before Me (God) for the land, that I should not destroy it, but I found no one" **Ezek. 22:30**. Through intercession, you can take the offensive in the spiritual battle, building up your community, your nation, and your world. As you follow God's call to rise up and take your place in the spiritual battle, God promises to "heal their land" **2 Chron. 7:14.**

JOINING THE BATTLE
God is calling Christians to join His battle plan for this world -- to join in intercessory prayer.

He is not looking for perfect prayer warriors, just willing hearts who want to see God will come to pass on the earth. All you have to do is turn to the Lord in prayer: "Father, I come into your presence and ask you to give me the heart of the intercessor. Help me to be persistent in prayer until the breakthrough comes. Thank You for this powerful weapon of spiritual warfare -- and for your faithfulness in my life. In Jesus' name. Amen." **FIGHT OUR BATTLE** "We live in this world, but we don't act like its people or fight our battles with the weapons of this world. Instead, we use God's power that can destroy fortresses. We destroy arguments and every bit of pride that keeps anyone from knowing God. We capture people's thoughts and make them obey Christ" **2 Cor. 10:3-5**.

The Shield for Spiritual Battle

I will lift up my eyes to the hills – from whence comes my help? My help comes from the Lord, who made heaven and earth. He will not allow your foot to be moved; He who keeps you will not slumber. Behold, He who keeps Israel shall neither slumber nor sleep. The Lord is your keeper; the Lord is your shade at your right hand. The sun shall not strike you by day, nor the moon by night. The Lord shall preserve you from all evil; He shall preserve your soul. The Lord shall preserve you're going out and your coming in from this time forth, and even forevermore."

Psalm 121:1 "… Deliver me speedily; be my rock of refuge, a fortress of defense to save me. For Christ Jesus You are my rock and my fortress; therefore, for your name's sake, lead me and guide me. Pull me out of the net which they have secretly laid for me, for Christ Jesus You are my strength. Into Your hand I commit my spirit; Christ Jesus You have redeemed me, O Lord God of truth."
Psalm 31:2 "Oh, how great is your goodness, which you have laid up for those who fear you, which you have prepared for those who trust in you in the presence of the sons of men! You shall hide them in the secret place of your presence from the plots of man; you shall keep them secretly in a pavilion from the strife of tongues."

Psalm 31:19 "The Lord is my light and my salvation; whom shall I fear? The Lord is the strength of my life; of whom shall I be afraid? When the wicked came against me to eat up my flesh, my enemies and foes, they stumbled and fell. Though an army should encamp against me, my heart shall not fear; though war should rise against me, in this I will be confident." **Psalm 27:1** "The Lord is on my side; I will not fear. What can man do to me? The Lord is for me among those who help me; therefore I shall see my desire on those who hate me. It is better to trust in the Lord than to put confidence in man. It is better to trust in the Lord than to put confidence in princes.

All nations surrounded me, but in the name of the Lord I will destroy them." **Psalm 118:6** "If God is for us, who can be against us?" **Romans 8:31** "God is our refuge and strength, a very present help in trouble. Therefore we will not fear, though the earth is removed, and though the mountains are carried into the midst of the sea ... God is in the midst of her, she shall not be moved; God shall help her, just at the break of dawn. **Psalm 46:1** "Whenever I am afraid, I will trust you. In God I will praise His word, in God I have put my trust; I will not fear. What can flesh do to me? ... In God I have put my trust; I will not be afraid. What can man do to me?" **Psalm 56: 3, 11** "When they went from one nation to another, from one kingdom to another people, He permitted no one to do them wrong;

Yes, He reproved kings for their sakes, saying "Do not touch my anointed ones, and do my prophets no harm." **Psalm 105:13** "Give us help from trouble, for vain is the help of man. Through God, we will do valiantly, for it is He who shall tread down our enemies." **Psalm 60:11** "For the Lord God will help me; therefore I will not be disgraced; therefore I have set my face like a flint, and I know that I will not be ashamed. He is near who justifies me; who will contend with me? Let us stand together. Who is my adversary? Let him come near me. Surely the Lord God will help me; who is he who will condemn me? Indeed they will all grow old like a garment; the moth will eat them up." **Isaiah 50:7** those who trust in the Lord are like Mount Zion, which cannot be moved but abides forever.

As the mountains surround Jerusalem, so the Lord surrounds His people from this time forth and forever." **Psalm 125:1** "Oh, bless our God, you peoples! And make the voice of His praise to be heard, who keeps your soul among the living, and does not allow our feet to be moved." **Psalm 66:8** "Even to your old age, I am He, and even to gray hairs I will carry you! I have made, and I will bear; even I will carry, and will deliver you." **Isaiah 46:4** "He who dwells in the secret place of the Most High shall abide under the shadow of the Almighty. I will say of the Lord, "He is my refuge and my fortress; my God, in Him I will trust. Surely He shall deliver you from the snare of the fowler and from the perilous pestilence.

He shall cover you with His feather, and under His wings, you shall take refugee; His truth shall be your shield and buckler. You shall not be afraid of the terror by night, nor of the arrow that flies by day, nor of the pestilence that walks in darkness, nor of the destruction that lay waste at noonday. A thousand may fall at your side, and ten thousand at your right hand; but it shall not come near you. Only with your eyes shall you look, and see the reward of the wicked. Because you have made the Lord, who is my refuge, even the Most High, your habitation, no evil shall befall you, nor shall any plague come near your dwelling; for He shall give His angels charge over you, to keep you in all your ways. They shall bear you up in their hands, lest you dash your foot against a stone.

You shall tread upon the lion and the cobra, the young lion and the serpent you shall trample. Because he has set his love upon me, therefore I will deliver him; I will set him on high because he has known my name. He shall call upon me, and I will answer him; I will be with him in trouble; I will deliver him and honor him. With long life, I will satisfy him, and show him my salvation." **Psalm 91:1-16** truth or judgment falls? It is because He is omnipotent (all-powerful) and in complete control that we know He will Fight for His people.

Intercession

Romans 8:26-34 in the same way, the Spirit helps us in our weakness. We do not know what we ought to pray for, but the Spirit himself intercedes for us through wordless groans. And he who searches our hearts knows the mind of the Spirit, because the Spirit intercedes for God's people in accordance with the will of God. And we know that in all things God works for the good of those who love him, who have been called according to his purpose. For those God foreknew he also predestined to be conformed to the image of his Son, that he might be the firstborn among many brothers and sisters. And those he predestined, he also called; those he called, he also justified; those he justified, he also glorified.

\

Salvation through the Blood of Jesus

Faith that can stand the test and pay the price and obey is Jesus Christ. And, God, thank You for giving us even that faith. We bless you for the blood of Jesus Christ, shed for the remission of sin, for the scarlet stream that flowed from His side, from His wounds, from His head, an outpouring of love, an outpouring of wrath, life for those who believe death for those who don't believe. We thank You, Father, that in Christ there is forgiveness, even for the unworthy such as we are.

And now, Lord, as we come to your table we ask that you would help us, to see the meaning of the cross all over again. And, Lord, if there's anyone reading this book who has not received Jesus Christ, who has not believed in Him as Lord and Savior, may they do that this moment. May they open their heart and receive the Son of God, accepting His death and resurrection as the only means to escape judgment and enjoy the blessings of eternal salvation.

Father, we pray also for those of us who have received Christ that we might be cleansed at this moment from any sin. We can be certain that Rahab through faith, through being identified with the people of God walked away from the sorted life of the past, eventually was included as a child of the living Savior Jesus Christ.

O Father, may it be that those of us who have placed faith in Jesus Christ too walk away from the sorted past and leave behind any sin and stain. Help us to confess now any known sin that we might truly celebrate your death with a clean heart. As human beings, we have a tendency to hold onto things. We like to maintain control and power over our lives, relationships, work, reputation, possessions, and just about everything else! We have a hard time embracing our vulnerable humanity and letting go. The good news that this story points to is the truth that we can stop trying to play God, and surrender our lives to Christ in Faith. Through our faith, Christ can turn our life around.

God Can Deliver

May God that suspended the stars in the sky and made the moon to shine; The God that gives us light by day and darkness by night; The God that woke you up this morning; He can do the very thing that you feel you can't do and remove from your life that very thing you feel you cannot get rid of that same God can move it and free you from this bondage. All God asks that you believe that his son Christ Jesus die for us and that he have all power in his hands and the gates of hell will not prevail. Ask Christ Jesus to come in your life today wherever you stand or set; Say Christ Jesus I want to be saved and I repent of my sins and ask you to forgive me; I am asking you to come into my life and be my Savior and I give my heart and soul to you on this day. I'm a living witness that Christ Jesus will reach out and touch your life he did it for me and I know he will do the same for you.

    Your Sister in Christ Jesus

DEDICATION

I dedicate this book to my sister Evangelist Wanda Denise Ayers an awesome Woman of God who gave up on the Fight and I hope that she knows that she is so precious in God sight. I remember how she laid her hand on our big brother Prophet Wilbert Ayers Jr. and he was touched by the Holy Spirit. How she prayed for our kids and God has kept them safe. I want her to know I miss all the laughter and fun times and looking forward to these amazing times again. I hope that something in this book will bring back the fight in her. Bringing her back to the warrior the fighter she once was. I know I do not say it enough but I Love you so very much.......

Your Sister with Love Carolyn

Jesus Christ is only a prayer away.

www.ingramcontent.com/pod-product-compliance
Lightning Source LLC
Chambersburg PA
CBHW032137040426
42449CB00005B/280